White
Piano

Nicole Brossard

translated by Robert Majzels and Erín Moure

Coach House Books, Toronto

first English edition

English translation copyright © Robert Majzels and Erín Moure, 2013

Original French text copyright © Nicole Brossard, 2011

Originally published in 2011 in French as *Piano blanc* by Les Editions
L'Hexagone

We acknowledge the financial support of the Government of Canada, through
the National Translation Program for Book Publishing, for our translation ac-
tivities. Coach House Books thanks, for their support, the Block Grant Pro-
grams of the Canada Council for the Arts and the Ontario Arts Council. We
also appreciate the support of the Government of Ontario through the Ontario
Book Publishing Tax Credit and the Government of Canada through the
Canada Book Fund.

LIBRARY AND ARCHIVES CANADA CATALOGUING IN PUBLICATION

Brossard, Nicole, 1943-
[Piano blanc. English]
        White piano / Nicole Brossard ; translated by Robert Majzels and Erin
Mouré. ~ 1st English ed.

Poems.
Translation of: Blanc piano.
ISBN 978-1-55245-273-8

        I. Majzels, Robert, 1950- II. Mouré, Erin, 1955- III. Title. IV. Title:
Piano blanc. English.

PS8503.R7P51813 2013   C841'.54   C2012-908532-4

This title is available as an ebook: ISBN 978 1 77056 345 2

We have to confront our own variation.

– Michel Serres

1

it's a quiet Wednesday
no one clamours
light reaches the body
coils round the wrists
darkness held in custody

2

softly we talk
of slipping toward the brink
disfigured
far from humanity

3

in the morning I've a number in my feelings
an eye of second person plural
a notion with me fed by emotion
by animal kingdom and by *azul*

4

now you watch out for the commas
that erase and raise the night
now when the time comes you caress
a sheet of water and its logic of conflagration

5

I say what they say
about not telling lies
it's infinitely
risky, and we breathe

6

one hour before summer
night had a body
as in certain phrases
at the edge of the universe

7

language I'll say yes
from the top of my rib cage
language will you come
out and unearth the salt the certitude

The Use of Tiny Vertigos

whoever still insists on clinging to the real
to stammer in the repertoire
of guns and the serial loops of others
upright our body doesn't think any less
sea, hunger, the mysterious manoeuvre
of air and its fabulous leaps in the chest
at the speed of shadow
to break free of the self you have to toe the line
between centuries and galaxies celestial hopscotch

our mythology of millennial night
a few names of beasts with hearts ripped out
fruity transparency of our sexes

it all breaks free of the self alive too brief

The Inside of Someone

I say the inside of someone not knowing
out of what muscle bone or ligament
if it's a line of horizon in the brain
or knots of night in the throat
not knowing if it's tender
or vast word with a name

The Inside of Someone: version2

first an idea of darkness
then I have hands
a few syllables jettisoned
but rough tide of morning returns
and the inner world is outspread
with shores of organic silence

The Inside of Someone: other version

okay so it's thick
with images of slow skiffs and cliffs
in the midst of dead languages
okay so too much absolute crashes in the gut

The Inside: version3

even if no one's there
the essential rolls eager with innards and infancy
draws its own lines of life
anecdotes not quite cannibal
even in the absence of pronouns
the essential absorbs the heat
of the frescoes of frenzy and confession

The Inside

without lux(ury) language strains unbearable
so I move quick
if we slow down if we erase I insist
I've just got to juggle
elsewhere slowly soaking softens me

come on narration I await
your indiscreet questions your ideas of *having a blast*
it's so simple, and pain we can recount
to substitute the carnivores

The Inside Reversed

grammar of echo round constellated
of peoples in flight,
city legs knees hurry up cited

then hope of superstition
a comfort of the end of the world

out there a rich foam of intimate life
spelled sky that thunders right up to the pupils

too much love and not enough
afterward we say it's the North
and we go to bed with a woman
in the silence slow foliage
we sleep right through the night
without punctuation or sepulchre
in the machine to inundate the world

suddenly I'm where the wind begins
I'd like to understand
mammals, the humanity that runs
in the veins
the hand-to-hand combat of grief
the drowned world the images of farewell
how our lips
and the huge side of the sea

other times it's suspicious I become
a generation a vine

a cascade of shadows and of dialogues

White Piano

Hotel Furama, L.A.

in the lounge white piano
a work in imagination
curled fingers centred over the keyboard
no night can live up to night and its story

Hotel Furama
the dictatorship rose up
all blue, all night
nuggets of interdiction

it would be dark
in a mirror at night it would be impossible
to lean close. To open our arms

every morning in the name of small survivals
the bougainvillea climb up to our knees;
later in the belligerent gleam of muscular
limos, we examine the ego

surveillance cameras and whirlpool baths
the Occident wavers
outside, a blue wind
uniforms
plastic chairs turned toward the void

between the lips small dexterous *I*s
by the thousands tormented
fists, palms primed for stones and backhand caresses

later, white piano
throat ardent, I know:
a life at the keyboard's well worth
the sincere shadow of a voice
right up to the eardrums the unfurling

why speak without shivers
the becoming of water the thought
of massacres
the silence framed field of light

as for the trees
that's all we do we count the rings
count up the bodies of women at dawn
particles of soul in the air

by the pool: we were saying here's a water
of America and of *takeoff*
here's a viable me
a devouring mouth in the heat wave

rest easy
the white piano soothes no one
in the absolute
we are very solo
with an intensity of *adieu*

'John Cage was interested in the piano as a percussion instrument, inserting various objects between the strings, such as screwdrivers, keys, coca-cola bottles,
in a technique called *prepared piano*'

it's a piano's shadow
ache smooth unceasing
of piano piano

Piano frontera

the vultures had already eaten her tongue and eyes

— a witness

fence we called it barbed wire
wall or whisper to me
also another phrase
between here and over the border
I still have a head on my shoulders

from the other side of the rio the sun licks
an eye, perfect
traverse it we must
between crosses and nails
bouquets of irises *no una de más*

Eyelids 1

her mouth plays dead while blood
trickles in the dust of a vacant lot
her mouth makes nO sound
not even a coagulated gesture
lightly on what's left of *lipstick*

almost not dead
just a palpitation a word snagged
in the soft fold of the cheek we all have
a word caressed with the tongue
like a sliver of pepper, ire

Eyelids 2

we don't say eyes anymore
an eye here eye that shines lurking
slave amid glints of prose

Eyelids 3

you still have your head
it happens every day
with blood that streams in decline
routine of round bellies
piled up just before death
anyway you can count

Eyelids1

your mouth's full of thirst
still you breathe
piano massacre of teeth
the mouth in front of you does it whisper
yes, or unspeakable springs to mind
in the damp crimson mix of seconds

the eyes, the lips: more blood
you enter the nO sound
the mouth is immobile
abyss, you feel the urge to leap
images too of vital organs

Eyelids2

the eye's no longer shaped like an eye
neither yours nor hers
her eye moves like an eye
as soon as you compare
it's no longer an eye

iris the word doesn't apply
only cornea
all the rest is torn up
on the brink of sinking
into nO noise
the chasm of the face

Eyelids3

don't confuse head and face
from up close it's round easier
with hair bolting horses reared up
but for the neck knocked red to the ground

Eyelids I

all night the mouth pulses
respiratory solution
its own heat is what keeps it moist
with cold-blooded sincerity
that hems between dialogues

Eyelids II

now the eye's in the nO
urge to somersault
in space a slow crevice anticipates
its own erasure

Eyelids III

half a life, half a sonata
white panic piano
you repeat: this is nonetheless a head
a woman's head round as a planet
from ankles to wrists to eyelids
you enter the nO nothing of being

Eyelids (mouth)

eyelids are no longer up to the task
bouquet of *lipstick*, her mouth cut
from all story stream universal
in the tiny background of numbers

Eyelets (eye)

from the other side of the phrase
the eye is a border eye
fear and its damp have unravelled
the eye of prose right up to cosmic blue

Eyelids (head)

we had to shut our eyes
in front of you a head *una de más*
line of abyss
between the throat and nape the nape

We wear Mortality
As lightly as an Option Gown
Till asked to take it off –
                              – Emily Dickinson

Piano Topology

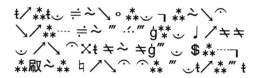

Every language when we breathe it is
brief as we say my mother to the depths
of return

in each language our violence is intact
we inhale it with its collisions
its t/errors and small print
then in 3steps in a *Neues* museum
stroke of the bow
an image deflects our attention

in reality reading helps us vanish
the everyday self from words reborn
there where once we left as dust
anonymous in the mystery of breaths
or in a book line skipped typo erased

no language rests in the universal

sooner or later between our lips all languages
all tongues sift darkness

scraps of refrains
wall whispers it's still
Berlin with risks of error and errantry
between the Gropius Museum and the Topography
of Terror

from there see the short man in glasses
a white skull on his cap
we see clearly that the city is a place
big enough for 60million faces
and a whiff of cosmos

and always the idea that in the distance
versatile it's our fertile life
still credible
our way of breathing

at first language goes right through us
with a little monkey tremor
curious
cloaked in absence we know it, it leaps

alpha*brat* deceiver
of arms and repeated legs
all day Sunday, and days of invention

every language cultivates its own craters of fire
its wells of flavours and consent
a crazy number of lessons abbreviated in our chests

as for our body
do we really speak by simulating
head tipped over opposite of anguish
do we speak reciprocal
body hunched in its hunt for breathing

this morning language transformed
my mammal intentions
into one idea two lives exploded
in the chest
under my warm coat
one hour later of melancholy
all along the Spree
piano bang of keys in the arteries

we'll foresee the sapidity of blood rolled in our 5senses
and xtimes the flavour: juniper clove mint viburnum
as for our body no one knows if it still wants
to speak fruits or white piano up to the brow
to soak in history
softly
sink into what follows and the silk lamé of the horizon

Paragraphs of Eternity

... where there are no sentences, there is no truth ... The world is out there, but descriptions of the world are not.
— Richard Rorty, *Contingency, Irony, and Solidarity*

We are made for eternity, but we do not know why.
— Elfriede Jelinek, *Jackie*

She did not want to float or swallow
or fall from a bridge, she did not want to
but she wanted because art,
the water of before and after
she walked long nights
in the calles among the works of ech.o

first image: vertical valour
500centuries of liquid light
she: arms extended torso hunched over
a water turned toward the sky
the colour of ink of algae
of impossible appeasement

warmth's origin, July
of all proper names in weightless state
I vow a clarity so sharp the iris shatters
sometimes right to Vicenza

she came in silence
existing with a notebook or her camera
in the halls of archives floored in wood
we quickly admitted an obsession we loved
to repeat: here we live well
under the vaulted ceiling and fresco by Titian

from the window the canal water blind

an encyclopedia of bridges and clouds
bright lively beam of molecules in the light
: water that frightens: stop moving

at noon life tells its story in spirals of raw light
in her eyes, smooth yet imaginary
a cartouche of eternity she might have concealed
in her hair and caressed

at cocktail hour limoncello
all eyes turn toward the horses
we contemplate the Orient
it will take many centuries more
to erase the furor
of those four horses, the copy

when the water rises, she telephones
the moon turns in its cone of shadow
if I hunch down I can caress with my finger
these images in the form of silver prints
where sometimes a traveller dozes
her face fingered by wind
she says: this is devious landscape
we will have to count our belongings

tsunami of words
with your palm you wanted to reverse
fear you wanted it just
as the vaporetto arrived

art unfolds sketches of night
deceptive pronoun effects
art raises the rebellious side
of words scolded in Emma's head

once again we thought of all that water fleeing
we spoke of tables overturned
of crimson dresses gone to pink
under crumbling ceilings
anyway we had to let the light in

night vaporetto night *nyx* neon slow
at five in the morning dawn entered
slowly sank into the voice
into the chest raising
monochromes of identity

when light strikes the *I* of sudden bereavements
she holds it in suspension
above the abyss in a wave of ululations
Emma says this image is slow
for the pink of palaces on the grand canal
the lapping of water that aches in the skull
this image is still too slow in the mouth

in the end, it was enough to leave the foam alone
along the canals listen float not searching
any further, the inside of someone
the narration of small absolutes

end of November someone spoke of Chicago
of Grant Park and of history

that night she became crowd
Emma crossed 3times the Ponte dell'Accademia

she did not want to be this rivulet
of repetition
along a blue canal a little
before dusk
in the garden of a Museum or on YouTube
filming or knocking on
her own fibre-optic silence

a little Casanova kissed in the Florian:
she held her like a key in the conversation
keeping a certain distance with her words
so that *vous-même* surreptitiously broke her heart

the universe bordered memory everywhere.
She'd had twenty years to work back to the Erinyes
and to the Atridae; to re-encounter dragons chimaera
all the red of Carpaccio and the head of Holophernes
twenty years to tame her fertility
without hallucinating in the new world
to adapt her heart's rhythm
to all the nanotears and swells of melancholy

coffee steaming keyboard fingers
entire days she searches
for a link the paper the ego of echo
she can also boast
of paradoxes and *piercings*

to recover from the water of shrinking glaciers
from each inflection of life in the voice
how to dig refuge in the figures of the self
exit a hotel room
exposed to all the winds of harmony, and the void

she holds her hand up like some distant machine
that might nourish her, reflect her story
she holds it out in front, hand mask wolf
having seen all the hanged figures
of Goya, and the others often

she touches on all the questions
because an idea of happiness
she washes the hours with words
because flesh because one day it'll be necessary
to speak of meat and of happiness

she'd had 20years to learn the slippage
between the words women and reality
between universe and room of one's own
several times her body became lodged
in the word @*space*

initiating herself into enigmas and the living womb of women
twenty years to transcribe paragraphs of eternity
an intimacy of inkwash in the material of the present

all is tide night haunted
the t-shirt with a skull
no one had worn it
before you that evening mingled with perfume

it passed through the throat
everyone had a name
a little vibration recycled under the tongue
while rain touched the present

on Lido beach
water entered the mouth
burst of pure-blooded Lippizaners.
Then at a gallop you bolted to brush against time
in your chest, and joy.
You keep your tongue young.

a wall of images had to be confronted
women half-buried soon stoned
women nose cut off immense hole of darkness
Emma wavers camera in her grasp
from wordless suffering to the photo
from the photo to those minutiae of story
where you can never again make peace

now she tied her scarf of winter and of darkness
the words went off every which way
why am I so burdened
by shadow and by humanity *disculpe*
repertory of fine needles stuck to immensity

prose, she thought, form dressed in sorrow

Story

/ I didn't write the story, you know. It was to start in Montréal, across from Parc Lafontaine, with a woman looking out a hotel window. She's awaiting a manuscript she's contracted to translate in the next six months without knowing the author's name, sex or age. And maybe without even knowing what her mother tongue was, language of childhood and of babbling, of fever, laughter and cries sealed in the invisible. The contract says a manuscript of one hundred pages written by O. R.

I'd been promised the story, I was waiting for it. In the distance I could make out my fear. I kept the woman moving, as I do now, watching her walk in a Montréal crowd thirsty for jazz. She strolls down Jeanne Mance Street between the water fountains and the avalanche of sounds entwined in thoughts and the pianos of Satie, Honegger and Malipiero of Venice. Later, at nightfall, under fetish light of *lipstick* rouge, when we can make out shoulders and fragile napes, she'll reappear with her intelligent face and questions for the entire planet.

I'd been promised a story, it awaited me. Everywhere prose settled into my notebooks, into thoughts, it positioned its people, wove connections, knotted plots in my bed just before I fell asleep. It seemed able to soothe and give pleasure. I liked its seeming transparency, which compelled me to think with that little bit of cunning and stillness needed to mollify the winged silhouette of death. Then one morning, poetry resurfaced, adapting for a while to the prose that enveloped pretty much every detail in my head. Stories leaking the way water leaks, seeping into the presence or slightest burst of poetry.

Time passed. The grammar of the everyday won't let go. From now on, the poem absorbs the dust of prose and the very special ardour akin to the need to think in the flow of time /

Piano Prose

You

'Around 1900, the world was as full of pianos as it is full of cars today. The market was saturated; people bought an instrument simply because the piano next door had become intolerable and they preferred to produce their own noise.'

I tell you life is only good for living
it takes dialogues, that's all
quivering swearing I tell you
I'm scarcely twenty years old scarcely
a pronoun in my solitude
from before all the wars

subterfuge of plural
having all of you in my head
creates a strange distance
like a number that could carve
a tactile sensation into the alphabet
of repeatedly the same voice

you does not really distance
attracts sometimes if we extend both arms
palms poised to plunge deep
into the imagination and thorax

you rapid worn down while traversing
a century a catastrophe
gibbon teeth in the night
orality of pink dust and subtitles
oh| my living proofs

you know I caressed all that's needed
of life and sumptuous beasts
but spread your wings once again
and your shells of ego, all of you, take wing
right to fine thirst and breath ribbon

be here be this
nocturnal figures plummeting
between centuries and works
know how to slow down
or figure out how
the inside of someone can shift
to reign freely in the form of petals
another day streaming
phrases dawn-fresh without error

Without Story

without story, don't touch the ashes

1
on a pebble the light
does it keep pain at bay
forever
the threat of clenched fists
the obsession of tomorrow

2
knots of habit
we were saying speed
invisible tears
or the dust has ribbons

3

without story we repeat
ankles, my head burns
epidemic,
we can only repeat my mother
breast or I, without story we need
the present, the light

4

without story no spilt wine
nor conversation nor caress that swims
and rosy contour around the fingers
nor photo of you who wanted
naked, brief and full of oxygen

5

without story fear rises
together crumbles fast
between the migrations
wild bursts of look-at-me
without story carpet of opacity out to infinity

6

without story heat of noon or face
the abyss wells up everywhere
it's too fast the last breath

7

without story who'll still want to lick
the vague matter at the origin of thoughts
the terror harpooning the body from the waist down,

8

without story continents dwindle
leaving only our lives slow to become lives
without pili-pili to reverse the pain
in the darkness of savoir-vie

Ultrasound

stubborn backbone
that chafes the depth of thoughts

in the plupresent of fear and ecstasy
in the simple present of our intelligent tissues

anon a landscape that rises like an ancient beast
flexible from throat to sex capable of flight and sudden
plunges of inebriate blue

the present wants the present up to the ears
then pain marks who is present; in the distance, cicadas
phrases unfurled 2ice without infinitive

at the time of the best sketches of solitude

to talk no more of coffins and repetition
laments language or quick the eyes above all
to displace the wind, the chic distresses. No one dares
laugh at themselves now because of fragile pronouns
with all our being we head toward elsewhere
to dip the alphabet in new mysteries
simple certainty of shadow
forever in the breast we carry a species overwhelmed
the pain of sincere wishes exchanged in chaos

so we clean the keyboard with our fingers
we disperse slowly solo
each crevice each key certain evenings
to speak in prose to speak dissipates the drownings of origin,

you've seen there are rhinestones
breezes too I was saying who
camouflages what

everyone wanted to enter consciousness
to meddle in the tiniest atoms of frenzy
on the brink of death everyone rolled their anguish
auto marble dice voice the same voice in a loop
to the end of love

       *

here I started to think again of Venice,
of ordinary scenes from Tiepolo, life of clay

piano and wise songs of water
amid touch screens where
question of instinct

we had to mix tastes,
languages, silks linen
tissue of intrigues
in the evening dig into the universe

cascade of ubiquity
no accumulation
a single longevity

maybe we're true, maybe on the contrary we're tomorrow
how to know if what comes
arises from deep in the throat from a double carnivore tumult
from a supple wrenching into the energy of the cosmos
maybe we're true. The pain is still whole

      *

nervous depth of sensations
from the anecdote to the others, time flays

we live in the flow of time, don't we
all these sofas sheets and beds where bodies are laid

Streaming

let the fires rage, breathlessness revolt

The universe is transparent toward the future
— Hubert Reeves, *Atoms of Silence*

the power of questions
if you sit at the piano
amid whirlwinds designed
to make us vanish

what on earth was I thinking
to touch like this
the continuous murmur of lives compared
our centre of gravity feverish
the carmine powders of sudden wind

back then, we did not understand
today we know
one sex every month, a sex
hidden in the versatile pink that swallows
the time of petals

don't be afraid
tomorrow won't drown tomorrow
or 2narratives gallop between the pupils
the present erodes memory
the very speed of absence

knowledge shifted swallowing origin
vocabulary and night
each swan
our rose endurance through the centuries

I also noticed that we'd added
to the heart and the everyday
minor lacerations that mark
without embrace or snares
so I entered another era
with skulls and all that in the grass
because au revoir we loved
nature and to lie down there

I let go repeating
with a body a soul and another verb.

I'm broken: rivers music and seaways.
I tow a dawn of eviscerated language
stuck to the great crushed totality of history.

I let go dying

in the distance memory emp/tied
of sea and wind by screens
I walk absorbed by the augmented reality
in all the angles of *singularity*

we'll soon find out if
all that happens is necessary
the depths of love that stream
other depths made for survival

thoughts cries and antiquity
in a single gulp of the present
embroiled in exquisite night
we'll soon find out if other
retorts if the others
will mount in mirrors
old goodbyes discharged
between characters, trompe-
l'œil
joy of illusion

we'll soon find out if the iris if it will all fly
right to Vicenza

Shade of the Ephemeral Without Familiarity

all this energy
mass of silence
obstinately feverish

almost, our death often
revives language
recomposes
without distance and without avowal
our nature

Streaming (continued)

between roots and ravines
sadness has tenderness
freefall of the living self
from under the void

we'll soon find out if the pain
if silence if fervour at the turning point
if the trampling the upper calves
if a 'tremulous ladder of tears'*
streams beyond naming

*Federico García Lorca, quoting Juan Calimacho

I let go dying
perfection change

following in my wake: water fountains glaciers
muqarnas under the celestial vault
pink hip of the muquères
friendship, my heart awash *duende*
also those rare dangers that enthrall
in a single navigation

I let go dying
what will we bring into existence
that's stark naked beyond breathing

several *longtime*
heat of your skin, aorta waiting
in time ready to pounce

done dying language embroiled in the bones
clouds of small aches that trap in mid-flight
space vaulted in its angles of purity

Streaming

the volcano, will we talk again
of nanomarbles of glass
of their invisible slowness abysmal until they reach us
will we talk again of all the metals we brush against
in the name of music and perfection

I touch on all the questions
I bathe the hours
because flesh because one day we must
speak of meat and of happiness

I let go dying
the yourselves and digital dialogues

eyes charged with an intensity of *adieu*
manuscripts of ephemera in plain sight
each of us swept up in our joy will glide
fingers keyboard clamour
in the night of savoir-vie

About the Author

Nicole Brossard is a poet, novelist and essayist who has published more than thirty books since 1965, including *These Our Mothers*, *Lovhers*, *Mauve Desert* and *Baroque at Dawn*. She has won two Governor General's Awards for poetry, as well as le Prix Athanase-David and the Canada Council's Molson Prize. Her most recent collection in English, *Notebook of Roses and Civilization*, also translated by Robert Majzels and Erín Moure, was nominated for the Griffin Poetry Prize. She lives in Montreal.

About the Translators

Erín Moure is a poet and translator from French, Spanish, Galician and Portuguese; she has published seventeen books of poetry. Her work has received the Governor General's Award, the Pat Lowther Memorial Award, the A. M. Klein Prize, and has been a three-time finalist for the Griffin Poetry Prize. Her most recent book of poetry is *The Unmemntioable* (2012).

Robert Majzels is a novelist, poet, playwright and translator. He is the author of the full-length play *This Night the Kapo* (Playwrights Canada Press), and four novels, most recently *Apikoros Sleuth* (The Mercury Press, 2004) and *The Humbugs Diet* (The Mercury Press, 2007).

Typeset in Albertan and Sympathique.

Albertan was designed by the late Jim Rimmer of New Westminster, B.C., in 1982. He drew and cut the type in metal at the 16pt size in roman only; it was intended for use only at his Pie Tree Press. He drew the italic in 1985, designing it with a narrow fit and very slight incline, and created a digital version. The family was completed in 2005 when Rimmer redrew the bold weight and called it Albertan Black. The letterforms of this type family have an old-style character, with Rimmer's own calligraphic hand in evidence, especially in the italic.

Printed in January 2013 at the old Coach House on bpNichol Lane in Toronto, Ontario, on Zephyr Antique Laid paper, which was manufactured, acid-free, in Saint-Jérôme, Quebec, from second-growth forests. This book was printed with vegetable-based ink on a 1965 Heidelberg KORD offset litho press. Its pages were folded on a Baumfolder, gathered by hand, bound on a Sulby Auto-Minabinda and trimmed on a Polar single-knife cutter.

Edited for the press by Susan Holbrook
Designed by Alana Wilcox
Cover image, *Missa*, by Dominique Blain, courtesy of the artist and the
    Meyers/Bloom Gallery, as photographed by Robert Wedemeyer.

Coach House Books
80 bpNichol Lane
Toronto ON M5S 3J4
Canada

416 979 2217
800 367 6360

mail@chbooks.com
www.chbooks.com